essential careers™

CAREERS AS A
PARALEGAL
AND LEGAL ASSISTANT

G. S. PRENTZAS

ROSEN
PUBLISHING®

NEW YORK

Published in 2014 by The Rosen Publishing Group, Inc.
29 East 21st Street, New York, NY 10010

First Edition

Library of Congress Cataloging-in-Publication Data

Prentzas, G. S.
Careers as a paralegal and legal assistant/G. S. Prentzas.
    p. cm.—(Essential careers)
Includes bibliographical references and index.
ISBN 978-1-4777-1790-5 ((library binding))
1. Legal assistants—Vocational guidance—United States. I. Title.
KF320.L4P735 2014
340.023'73—dc23

                                                                                2013012399

Manufactured in Malaysia

CPSIA Compliance Information: Batch #W14YA: For further information, contact Rosen Publishing, New York, New York, at 1-800-237-9932.

contents

INTRO

A paralegal conducts an interview. Paralegal work involves interviewing, performing legal research, and carrying out many other legal tasks under the supervision of a licensed attorney.

DUCTION

L ife in modern society seems to become more complex every day. This complexity results in an increase in both the number and types of legal disputes. A borrower fails to repay a lender. A landlord does not keep his property in good condition, making it unfit for a tenant. An employer discriminates against an employee. A car wreck injures a driver. Police arrest a person for allegedly breaking the law.

Although attorneys have become an easy target for criticism and the butt of many jokes, they provide vital legal services to individuals and organizations. They help people resolve legal disputes. They file lawsuits to help clients recover damages. They represent defendants in criminal trials. They provide legal advice and draft contracts, wills, and other legal documents needed by their clients. Attorneys work in private legal practices, law firms, corporations, government agencies, and in many other organizations and fields.

To help provide effective and efficient legal services, many attorneys, law firms, and legal departments hire paralegals. The American Bar Association (ABA) defines a paralegal, or legal assistant, as "a person . . . who is employed . . . by a lawyer, law office, corporation, governmental agency or other entity and who performs specifically delegated substantive legal work for which a lawyer is responsible."

Paralegals use their training, background, and experience to perform some legal tasks that have traditionally been performed by attorneys. Paralegals are not legal secretaries, who answer phones, file, and perform other clerical duties. A paralegal performs substantive legal work. That means their tasks require evaluating, organizing, analyzing, and communicating facts and legal concepts. Most people in the legal services industry consider "paralegal" and "legal assistant" to be the same position. Consequently, for the purposes of this career study, the word "paralegal" is used to represent both terms.

The legal services field shrank following the 2007–2008 financial crisis. As the economy recovered, however, law firms began enlarging their support staffs. The prospects for people interested in pursuing a paralegal career remain strong. Employment experts predict that the demand for paralegal services will likely rise more quickly than the demand for jobs in many other fields. Because paralegals earn lower pay than attorneys, many law firms and legal departments are expanding their paralegal staffs while reducing the number of attorneys they employ. Hiring paralegals to perform legal tasks helps lower the cost of legal services for clients.

Paralegal jobs are available in most areas of the country. A paralegal career offers increased responsibilities as a paralegal gains experience. It also provides the opportunity to specialize in many different legal fields, such as corporate law, criminal law, and environmental law. Working as a paralegal can offer an interesting, fast-paced career. A paralegal career may also provide the satisfaction of helping people resolve their legal problems.

chapter 1

THE LEGAL SERVICES INDUSTRY

L aws are the established rules of conduct in a society. They define the rights and duties of citizens. They enable people to predict the legal consequences of their actions. In the United States, lawyers and law firms provide legal advice and representation to their clients. The legal services industry helps individuals, corporations, non-profit organizations, governments, and other types of clients resolve their legal issues and disputes.

THE U.S. LEGAL SYSTEM

When the United States declared its independence from Great Britain in 1776, the thirteen states established a new governing body, known as the Continental Congress. Each state sent delegates to meetings of the Continental Congress. A committee of these delegates drafted an agreement intended to govern the new nation. This document, the Articles of Confederation, gave most governmental authority to the states. The delegates created a weak central government on purpose. Although all the states did not ratify, or approve, the Articles of Confederation until 1781, the states and the Continental Congress followed the principles set out in the document.

The United States won its independence in 1783. The weak central government created by the Articles of Confederation was not working well, however. The states were arguing with one another over commerce and other issues. In 1787, delegates from the thirteen states met in Philadelphia to revise the Articles. After much discussion, they instead drafted a new document, the U.S. Constitution.

The U.S. Constitution divides the responsibilities of government between a national, or federal, government and the governments of the states. It grants certain powers to the federal government and reserves all other powers for the states. By 1790, all of the states had ratified the U.S. Constitution. One year later, ten additional provisions, known as amendments, were added. These original amendments to the U.S. Constitution are known as the Bill of Rights. They guarantee freedom of speech, due process, and other individual rights and liberties. Today, each of the fifty states has a state constitution. Although some differences exist, the constitutions of the states are similar to the U.S. Constitution.

The U.S. Constitution is the nation's supreme law. That means no state constitution, federal or state statute, regulatory agency rule, or judicial opinion can conflict with it. The U.S. Supreme Court decides what

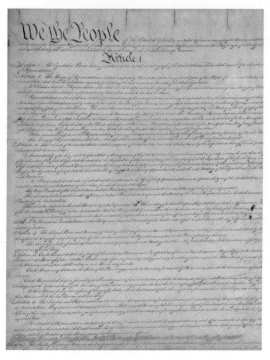

The U.S. Constitution is the central source of law in the United States. By assisting lawyers, paralegals serve an important role in the U.S. legal system.

the U.S. Constitution means. It has the power to invalidate any law or reverse any judicial opinion that violates the U.S. Constitution.

The federal and state constitutions are the basic sources of law in the United States. Federal and state statutes and administrative rules and regulations, adopted by federal or state government agencies and executive branches, are other sources of law. Congress and state legislatures empower various administrative agencies to regulate certain activities and enforce agency rules. For example, the U.S. Occupational Safety and Health Administration adopts and enforces regulations to ensure workplace safety.

The court system is the centerpiece of the U.S. legal system. Trial courts resolve legal disputes by allowing parties with opposing interests to present their arguments. The primary role of a trial court is to determine the facts of a dispute. For

In a courtroom, an attorney questions a witness as members of the jury look on. Paralegals sometimes assist attorneys during trials, preparing witnesses to testify and watching jurors' reactions to testimony.

example, in a case involving a car wreck, each side will present its version of the accident in court. Once the parties have presented their witnesses and other evidence, the judge then instructs the jury on the laws that apply to the case. The jury next decides the facts of the case and determines which party is at fault. For instance, the jury may decide that one of the

Attorneys and paralegals at a law firm discuss a client's case in a conference room. Paralegals often play a key role in providing legal services to a law firm's clients.

drivers caused the accident by running a red light. The court will issue an order for the at-fault driver to pay the damages suffered by the other driver.

Appellate courts hear appeals of trial court decisions. A losing party can appeal the verdict to an appellate court. Appellate courts determine whether the jury correctly applied the

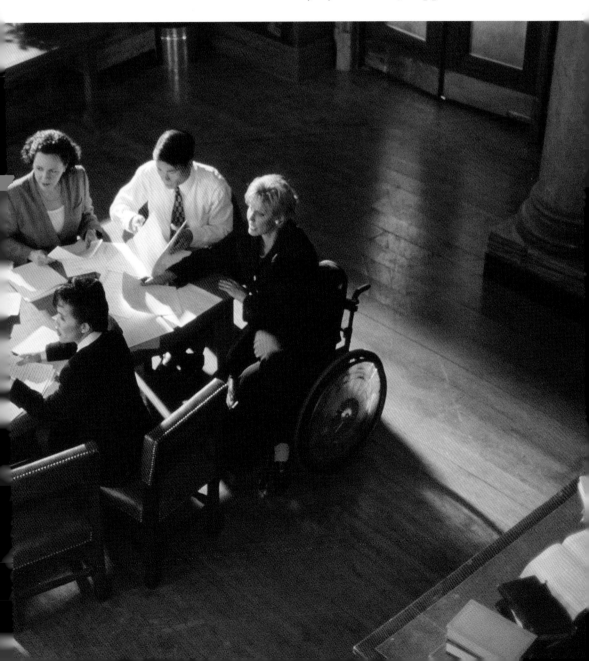

relevant legal principles to the facts of the case. If an appellate court overturns a decision, it returns the case to the trial court for a new trial.

THE PRACTICE OF LAW

The United States has an adversarial legal system. This type of system means that legal disputes are decided by opposing parties. The parties either negotiate an agreement, or settlement, to end the dispute, or they decide to go to trial to resolve their

A lawyer (left) consults with a paralegal. Attorneys assign legal tasks to paralegals and supervise their work. State statutes prohibit paralegals from practicing law, which includes providing legal advice or a legal opinion to another person.

dispute. For example, if a borrower fails to repay a loan, the lender can file a civil lawsuit against the borrower to recover the lender's money. When a prosecutor charges a person with a crime, a criminal case begins.

Attorneys provide legal services to parties in civil and criminal cases. They represent clients in negotiating the settlement of a civil dispute or a plea bargain in a criminal case. If a dispute goes to trial, an attorney presents his or her client's case to the court. Attorneys also provide legal advice to clients to help them avoid lawsuits or criminal charges. They also write legal documents, such as contracts and wills, to protect a client's legal and financial interests. The day-to-day tasks of attorneys differ greatly depending on the type of law the attorney practices.

THE STATE BAR

In all states, the only people who can legally practice law are attorneys who are members of the state's bar association. A state bar association is a professional organization of lawyers. Each state bar association requires an attorney to pass a competency test, known as a bar exam, before he or she can become a member. An attorney who is a member of a state bar can provide legal services in that state. State bar associations also adopt ethics and professional responsibility regulations that govern their members.

THE ROLE OF PARALEGALS

Paralegals play an important part in the U.S. legal system. They assist attorneys in providing legal services to clients. By law, an attorney must supervise the work of a paralegal. Unlike an attorney, a paralegal cannot provide legal advice or opinions to another person. Their role is limited to performing legal tasks that do not constitute the practice of law.

By performing a wide range of legal tasks that would otherwise be performed by an attorney, paralegals enable attorneys to focus on providing legal advice to their clients. Employing paralegals also enables attorneys, law firms, and legal departments to lower the cost of providing legal services to their clients. Many paralegals find satisfaction in their work because they enjoy working with people. Linda Omundsen, a paralegal who specializes in trusts and estates law, told *Paralegal Today* magazine, "I feel like I am contributing to something, like I'm helping people."

chapter 2

A Paralegal's Profession

Paralegals perform a wide variety of legal tasks assigned to them by an attorney. Paralegals are not legal secretaries, whose duties are usually limited to performing clerical and other office tasks. To become a paralegal, a person usually takes courses to earn a degree or certificate in paralegal studies. Once hired, paralegals learn how to perform legal duties directly from their employers. This type of learning is known as on-the-job training.

Attorneys, law firms, and other legal employers value paralegals because they complete tasks that an attorney would otherwise have to handle. Employing paralegals to perform certain assignments allows attorneys to focus on complex legal issues that require their expertise. It also offers attorneys more time to provide legal advice and opinions to clients. The use of paralegals for certain jobs also lowers the cost of providing legal services.

PARALEGAL WORK

Paralegals apply their legal knowledge and on-the-job training to perform legal tasks under the supervision of an attorney. Paralegals also provide additional types of support to their employers, including maintaining case files, conducting legal research, and drafting legal documents.

A paralegal (right) helps transport a large number of documents, which the attorney (left) will submit to a court. Paralegals often handle and organize many legal documents involved in a client's case.

Attorneys employ paralegals in many different ways, so the work of paralegals can vary greatly. A paralegal working in a large law firm may specialize in only one specific field, such as real estate. In contrast, a paralegal working for an individual practice may work on cases in many different fields, ranging from civil lawsuits to criminal defense.

In a small law firm or individual practice, a paralegal usually has a wider variety of responsibilities. These paralegals often work on a specific case from its beginning to its end. They may investigate and write a report on a potential client's issue before the firm takes on the case. They may even help prepare the legal arguments and draft documents to be filed with a court.

In larger law firms, a paralegal may primarily work on a specific phase of a client's case. For example, the paralegal may be responsible for filing documents with a court. Also at larger firms, an experienced paralegal may become a supervisor, overseeing a specific case and assigning work to other paralegals.

INVESTIGATIONS

Most legal cases revolve around the facts of a case. To give clients sound legal advice or to represent them effectively, an attorney must have accurate, thorough, and reliable facts. Assembling the facts of a specific case takes a lot of time in most instances. Attorneys often delegate fact gathering to paralegals. An investigation requires collecting and organizing information from different types of sources.

Interviewing is an important part of an investigation. For example, if a client is involved in a car accident, the paralegal will start by interviewing the client. She or he will record the client's version of the accident. The paralegal will also interview witnesses to get their versions of the accident. Interviewing requires patience and tact. A paralegal must be able to identify legally important facts and ask witnesses follow-up questions.

A paralegal (right) working for a civil rights organization interviews a day laborer. Conducting field investigations is a common task for many paralegals. They submit written reports summarizing the interviews to their supervising attorneys.

A paralegal may also have to conduct a field investigation to gather information essential to the client's case. For instance, the paralegal might visit the scene of the car accident to sketch an intersection, measure distances, or search for any video cameras that could have recorded the accident. The paralegal may also track down documents relevant to the case.

LEGAL RESEARCH

For many paralegals, a large part of their job is conducting legal research. Legal research is the process of finding the laws that apply to a specific legal issue. The goal of a paralegal's legal research is to locate the current laws that may apply to a legal issue, determine which laws apply to that issue, and summarize how the law affects the client's case.

Paralegals assist attorneys by performing basic legal research. In some instances, they may find and then organize the general legal principles that are relevant to the client's case. Other times they may conduct preliminary research on a specific, more complex legal issue.

Legal research requires a paralegal to examine many sources. Various sources may provide the laws relevant to a client's case. For a specific case, a paralegal may have to search federal and state laws, local laws, and government regulations. They may also need to research case law. Case law is made up of the written decisions of judges in past cases. Each state has its own case law, made up of decisions by courts in the state. The federal court system also has its own case law. Other legal resources, such as law encyclopedias and reference books, summarize current law.

Most attorneys and paralegals use computers to conduct legal research. Electronic resources allow researchers to search databases for specific laws, cases, or phrases. Westlaw, LexisNexis, and other online legal research services help researchers to identify quickly the laws and cases that apply to their client's case.

Paralegals' legal research must be accurate and thorough. They usually write a memorandum to the lawyer. The legal memo states the legal issue involved and the goal of the paralegal's research. It then provides a summary of known facts and identifies relevant statutes and court decisions. Attorneys use a paralegal's research to give clients advice or to prepare arguments to present in court on behalf of the client. Lawyers sometimes ask paralegals to summarize the impact of their research on the client's case. Interpreting the law and how the law applies to the facts of the client's case, however, is the attorney's role.

DOCUMENTS

Attorneys often assign tasks involving legal documents to paralegals. Under the supervision of an attorney, paralegals draft

A group of paralegals discuss a client's case. In larger law firms, paralegals often work as part of a paralegal team. Each paralegal may be assigned tasks involving only one aspect of a specific case.

Maintaining the Legal Calendar

court pleadings, contracts, wills, deeds, and other documents. To avoid ethical issues and the unauthorized practice of law, the supervisory attorney must review all legal documents prepared by a paralegal. Paralegals also write routine correspondence and internal memos.

Paralegals often handle physical documents, such as affidavits and other formal types of documentary evidence. Paralegals are also responsible for filing pleading, motions, and other paper documents with courts or delivering documents to clients or other attorneys. This aspect of a paralegal's job is becoming less common because most courts now accept electronic documents for many pleadings and motions.

Attorneys perform many legal services that involve deadlines. An attorney or law firm must file court documents by a certain date, answer a letter promptly, or ensure that contracts, wills, and other documents are signed in a timely fashion. In many law offices, paralegals are responsible for keeping track of deadlines and other dates paramount to clients. Paralegals must enter all important dates into a master calendar and establish procedures to make sure no deadlines are missed. A missed deadline could have serious consequences for a client.

Pretrial Preparation and Trial Assistance

Paralegals often help an attorney prepare for trial. They may interview witnesses, organize witness statements, and conduct additional investigations and legal research. They may also create exhibits or other visual aids, assemble questions to ask potential jurors, and prepare motions to be presented during the trial.

The use of technology is vital to trial preparation. Paralegals must learn to use computers and software to organize information and evidence for trial. Paralegal Patrick Rogan told *Paralegal Today* magazine, "You have to learn [how to use new technologies] if you want to be successful. Sometimes you have to show an attorney you can use technology to get organized and not get bogged down."

At trials and other legal proceedings, paralegals can perform certain tasks to assist an attorney. They may offer the attorney opinions during jury selection and watch jury members during the trial. They may be responsible for organizing and bringing files and evidence to the courtroom. They may take detailed notes of the proceedings. Except in certain cases allowed by statute, paralegals cannot represent a client in a legal proceeding.

During a trial, an attorney questions an expert witness about DNA evidence. Paralegals often help attorneys prepare for trials, including making charts, diagrams, and other visual displays.

CLIENT RELATIONS

A major aspect of a paralegal's work is client relations. Many of the tasks assigned to a paralegal involve working directly with the client. Paralegals often interview clients to get factual information. A paralegal is usually a client's primary contact at a law office. He or she keeps the client up to date on the progress of the case or project. A paralegal passes messages between the client and the supervising attorney. At trial, a paralegal explains the proceedings to the client and helps that individual relax. After a trial, a paralegal may monitor whether a court order affecting the client is followed or whether the client's bail payment is refunded.

chapter 3

PREPARING FOR A PARALEGAL CAREER

Paralegals perform crucial legal work that affects the outcome of clients' cases. Supervising attorneys assign paralegals work that they would have to perform themselves. To complete assigned tasks efficiently and effectively, a paralegal needs to have specific skills and personal traits to be successful. A person considering entering the paralegal field should analyze their skills and traits to determine if they are compatible with the career's requirements.

INVESTIGATIVE, RESEARCH, AND ANALYTICAL SKILLS

Paralegals are part of a team that provides legal services to clients. They must be able to apply their legal knowledge to help attorneys resolve their clients' legal problems. Analytical skills include the ability to use logic and reasoning, to solve problems, and to make good decisions based on facts. Paralegal work also requires independent thinking.

Paralegals must have good investigative and research skills. For many paralegals, conducting investigations and legal research on a client's legal problem is a major part of their job. If a client is divorcing a spouse, for instance, a paralegal may need to research statues and legal decisions relevant to the client's specific legal issue. If the couple is having a dispute over child custody, a specific issue could be whether a spouse's prior criminal conviction has an impact on which spouse gets custody of the child. A paralegal would research state law and court decisions in previous divorce cases involving criminal convictions and custody.

ORGANIZATIONAL SKILLS

Paralegals must have excellent organizational skills. They may work on just one case at a time or may be responsible for many cases simultaneously. They must organize their work to ensure that required tasks are completed promptly and manage their time wisely. Paralegal work involves many deadlines. Lawyers often rely on paralegals to make sure court documents and other legal papers are filed on time.

A paralegal searches the shelves of a law library. Conducting legal research into the statutes and court decisions relevant to a client's case is the primary task performed by paralegals.

An organized, efficient paralegal will likely advance in his or her career. Jean Cushman, a paralegal working in San Jose, California, observed in a *Paralegal Today* magazine article, "When attorneys see high-caliber paralegal work, they will automatically begin to think of that paralegal when passing out projects. Each project extremely well done will reap another [project]."

COMMUNICATION SKILLS

To perform their jobs, paralegals must be able to communicate in a professional manner, both in writing and speaking. Because of the nature of legal work, all documents and conversations must be factually correct. Paralegals must use legal terminology correctly and should convey information clearly. All written communications must use correct spelling, grammar, and punctuation. In both speech and written documents, a paralegal should avoid using slang, or informal language.

In law offices, most daily communications are written. A paralegal must present his or her research and related information to the supervising attorney in a clearly written, organized document. Paralegals often write interview and deposition summaries, investigation reports, and research memos. Paralegals also draft many types of legal documents, including wills, contracts, briefs, and court pleadings. They must also write letters and other documents to clients, other lawyers, witnesses, and other people involved in a client's case.

COMPUTER SKILLS

Computer technology has become an essential part of almost all law offices. Most legal documents are created on computers. Computers also help law offices keep track of important deadlines, such as trial dates and deadlines for court documents.

A paralegal uses a laptop to update information in a client's file. To perform their jobs effectively, paralegals must know how to use current computer technology and various software programs.

Most courts now require pleadings and other legal documents submitted to them to be in an electronic format.

Computers also help law offices organize information and data for clients and to present information and arguments to courts or regulatory agencies. A paralegal needs basic word-processing skills to write letters, memos, e-mails, and other communications. She or he also needs good computer skills to conduct online legal research, create spreadsheets, and use electronic databases. Many law offices use case management software and other types of software to organize and keep track of important information.

PERSONAL TRAITS

Paralegals must have specific personal traits to perform their demanding jobs effectively. A paralegal must be honest and loyal. When an attorney agrees to represent a client, he or she has an obligation to handle the client's case professionally. The attorney must keep the client's personal information in confidence and cannot place personal interests over his or her duty to the client's interests. A paralegal is held to the same standards of trust and honesty as an attorney. Paralegal

work requires loyalty, both to the supervising attorney and to the client.

Paralegals work closely with clients, witnesses, and other legal professionals. They must be able to forge good working

A paralegal (right) *interviews a potential witness. Because a paralegal often interacts with clients, witnesses, and other parties involved in a legal case, having good people skills is an essential trait for a paralegal.*

ADVICE FROM A PARALEGAL

Mary L. Creekmore has more than fifteen years of experience as a paralegal. She works for a law firm near Philadelphia and teaches legal studies courses at St. Joseph's University. Creekmore advises people considering a career as a paralegal that the most important skill for a paralegal is "the ability to prioritize and multitask." Paralegals usually have many tasks to complete every day. These tasks may involve working with several supervising attorneys on different cases that are in different stages. On a typical day, a paralegal deals with large amounts of information, ranging from legal research and documents to trial evidence and correspondence. According to Creekmore, working as a paralegal requires "critical thinking and superior reading comprehension."

Creekmore also identifies other skills paralegals need to succeed. They must be able to "think ahead and anticipate" what attorneys and clients need. They must be able to communicate effectively. She advises both aspiring and working paralegals that "honing your writing skills will increase your marketability."

Successful paralegals also have several indispensible personality traits. They can motivate themselves and handle complex tasks with little supervision. They are also flexible, meaning that they can change their priorities quickly or devote more time than anticipated on some projects. Creekmore points out perhaps the most important trait that will help paralegals excel: "A positive attitude will be your greatest key to success. Being positive empowers you to achieve your goals and gives you inner strength."

Source: Mary L. Creekmore, "Top Essential Skills and Assets for Paralegals." *Legal Intelligencer*, February 4, 2010. Retrieved March 21, 2013 (http://www.law.com/jsp/pa/PubArticlePA.jsp?id=120 2441952307&slreturn=20130221120856).

A paralegal (left) meets clients for the first time. Paralegals should convey professionalism at work, which includes being poised and dressing appropriately for client meetings, field investigations, and court appearances.

relationships with people. By using his or her interpersonal skills, a paralegal will be able to put a client or witness at ease while the person is sharing information relevant to the case. To do their job, paralegals must have compassion for people. They must be able to understand and respect a client's decisions, circumstances, and problems; this trait is known as empathy.

PROFESSIONALISM

Legal employers expect paralegals to conduct themselves as professionals at all times. Paralegals often work independently. They deal with a wide range of other people, from opposing counsel to witnesses and court employees. Professionalism requires a paralegal to display a self-confident attitude and a serious demeanor.

The most important aspect of paralegals' professionalism requires them to maintain confidentiality. When an attorney agrees to represent a client, the attorney takes on a duty of confidentiality. The attorney is obligated never to reveal any information received from a client to a third party without the client's permission. Paralegals have the same ethical obligation. They cannot mislay papers related to the client's case. They cannot gossip about the client or the case. They cannot allow their telephone conversations concerning the client's case to be overheard.

chapter 4

EDUCATION AND TRAINING PROGRAMS

Some paralegals do not have any formal education in paralegal studies. They learn the profession through on-the-job training provided by their employers. These paralegals usually already have a college degree. Many also have experience in a field related to law. For instance, a criminal defense lawyer may hire someone with a background in criminal justice, such as a former police officer, as a paralegal. A law firm specializing in health law may hire a nurse as a paralegal.

Most employers, however, require the paralegals they hire to have either a certificate or degree in paralegal studies. The National Federation of Paralegal Associations (NFPA) estimates that 85 percent of paralegals have specialized education or training. The United States has about one thousand colleges and private schools that offer paralegal education programs. The paralegal education field has no set program of study or educational standards. The ABA, however, accredits programs that meet its requirements. Fewer than three hundred paralegal programs have ABA accreditation.

Paralegal education typically includes courses on general legal subjects and on specific legal fields, such as real estate law. Some programs require additional general education courses, such as psychology or history courses. People seeking paralegal training can choose among four different types of educational programs.

CERTIFICATE PROGRAMS

Many community colleges, as well as some universities and colleges, offer paralegal certificate programs. Private educational institutions, such as technical and vocational schools, also offer certificate programs. These institutions often specialize in training programs in several varying fields. The Institute of Business and Medical Careers, for example, offers a paralegal certificate program. It also provides programs in business and health care.

Paralegal certificate programs vary in size, courses offered, and types of students. These programs usually take from four to eighteen months to complete. Some institutions offer day classes only. Others offer night and weekend classes. Certificate programs offering night and weekend classes are aimed at students who work during the week. Certificate programs are

A paralegal instructor conducts a classroom discussion. Paralegal employers usually require prospective employees to have a paralegal studies degree or certificate. A wide range of paralegal studies programs are available.

intended primarily for students who already have a college degree. Some programs, however, admit students who work in the legal field or who have only a high school degree. Students who complete a certificate program's requirements do not earn a degree. Instead, a student receives a certificate of achievement. The certificate acknowledges that the student completed the program's course requirements. The American Institute for Paralegal Studies posted a quote from a graduate of its certification program on its Web site. The graduate summarized the value of paralegal education, saying, "I feel more confident . . . as a paralegal. I actually understand the process, when the attorneys are talking about a deal."

Most certificate programs focus on providing a broad range of legal knowledge to students. Courses cover specific areas of law, such as business law or criminal law.

DISTANCE LEARNING

Many paralegal studies programs offer an option for distance learning. These online courses help students who cannot attend traditional classes to earn a certificate or degree. Distance learning is more common in certificate programs, but many colleges that grant associate's or bachelor's degrees offer online paralegal courses. Some schools offer their entire paralegal program online. At many schools, however, students can complete only certain courses online. Paralegal training programs that are approved by the ABA do not allow students to complete the entire paralegal program online.

To benefit from distance learning courses, students should have excellent computer skills and up-to-date equipment. They should also have the ability to work independently. Online courses are not as organized as classroom courses. Students must manage their own study.

Other common courses in certificate programs introduce students to legal terminology, court rules, and legal research. Longer certificate programs also require additional general education courses. Some shorter certificate programs do not offer courses that provide training for the practical aspects of paralegal work. For instance, a certificate program may not offer a course on drafting legal documents or operating computer software programs that are commonly used in the legal profession.

TWO-YEAR PROGRAMS

Students seeking paralegal education may also enroll in an associate's degree program. Associate's degree programs are usually two-year programs offered by community colleges. The Community College of Baltimore County, for example, offers an associate of applied science in paralegal studies degree. Some colleges and universities also offer associate's degrees in paralegal studies. The University of Louisville, for instance, offers an associate of arts degree in paralegal studies.

Many schools offering associate's degrees in paralegal studies develop their courses by seeking input from legal professionals. Local lawyers and paralegals, former students, and other experts in the legal field keep the school up to date on current practices in the paralegal field.

Associate's degree programs usually offer students a greater variety of courses than certificate programs. Most of these programs require courses on legal research, legal writing, and general legal principles. Students can take elective courses on specific legal topics, including business law, bankruptcy, family law, and personal injury law.

To prepare students for their careers, many associate's degree programs offer courses to help students build practical skills that paralegals use daily in their jobs. Students take courses in business communications, computers and software, and litigation basics. Most colleges also require paralegal studies students to take courses in subjects outside of the paralegal program. These courses range from literature and history to accounting and economics.

A paralegal studies student makes a classroom presentation. Paralegal studies programs provide students with basic legal knowledge and help prepare them for the practical aspects of a paralegal career.

The course work in an associate's degree program requires a lot of time and effort. Paralegal studies courses are challenging. Students must read a lot of course materials, complete assignments, and participate in classroom discussions. Legal courses require analytical and creative thinking, not just memorization. Students earn an associate's degree in paralegal studies when they complete all of the school's degree requirements.

Because of the number of people seeking paralegal training, admission to most associate's degree programs is competitive. Most colleges have specific admission requirements. A paralegal studies department may have additional admission requirements. Most associate's degree programs consider an applicant's high school grades and standardized test scores, such as the SAT. Some paralegal programs use preadmission interviews to select students. An admissions officer may ask the student why he or she is interested in a paralegal career and how that individual plans to use his or her paralegal studies training.

Students who want to pursue an associate's degree in paralegal studies should consider taking courses in high school or vocational school that build skills needed by a paralegal. History, sociology, and public-speaking courses will benefit students considering a paralegal career. Business, writing, and computer classes will also help prepare students for their paralegal studies and work.

FOUR-YEAR PROGRAMS

Some colleges and universities offer a paralegal bachelor's degree. Although most of these four-year institutions offer only a minor in paralegal studies, some have a paralegal studies major. Tulane University is one educational institution that offers a bachelor of arts degree in paralegal studies.

Four-year degree programs offer students a longer period of study than certificate or associate's degree programs. Paralegal students in these programs can choose from a wider range of courses. The paralegal curriculum in a four-year program includes introductory courses covering legal research, legal terminology, and legal ethics. More specialized courses include corporate law, health care law, and constitutional law.

Bachelor's degree programs also offer the advantages of a traditional four-year college education. To satisfy graduation requirements, students take courses in a wide assortment of college-level subjects, from math and science to psychology and foreign languages. The National Federation of Paralegal Associations urges prospective paralegals to earn a bachelor's degree. The organization believes that a bachelor's degree provides students a well-rounded education and prepares them for the challenges of modern paralegal work.

FINANCING PARALEGAL TRAINING

A paralegal education can be expensive. Many students must rely on financial aid to afford the training needed for a career as a paralegal. There are three major sources of financial aid. An educational loan is the most common type of financial aid. Through banks or government or school financial aid programs, a student borrows money to help pay tuition and other expenses. The student must repay the loan after graduation. Work-study programs provide students with part-time jobs so they can earn money to help pay for their education. Finally, grants and scholarships are types of financial aid that students do not have to pay back. Grants are usually awarded based on a student's financial need. Scholarships may be based on either merit, financial need, or a wide range of other factors.

Many four-year paralegal programs require students to complete an internship to graduate. Internships usually require paralegal students to gain practical work experience under the supervision of an attorney or other legal professional. For example, Eastern Michigan University requires paralegal studies students to complete a 150-hour internship. Assistant professor Nancy Cane Harbour noted in a *Paralegal Today* article, "Having hired and trained paralegals in the real world, I'm a big believer in teaching real-world skills to paralegal students." Degree programs requiring paralegal internships often match up students with local attorneys.

MASTER'S DEGREE PROGRAMS

A small percentage of paralegals continue their education and earn a graduate degree. Some universities offer a master's degree

Graduate paralegal studies students prepare for a class. Some universities offer master's degrees in paralegal studies in specialized fields. A master's degree provides additional credentials for a paralegal seeking employment in competitive areas of legal specialization, such as tax law.

in paralegal studies. George Washington University, for instance, offers a master's of science degree in paralegal studies. To qualify for a master's degree program, a student must have a bachelor's degree and submit a Graduate Record Examination (GRE) score to a school's admission office. Graduate paralegal programs usually require two years of study. Once admitted to a program, a student must pass a required number of courses, usually in such specialty fields as taxation or real estate. Master's degree students must also complete a lengthy thesis on a specific topic. The student usually must defend the thesis before a panel of faculty members. If the panel approves the thesis, the student earns a master's degree.

chapter 5

PROFESSIONAL REQUIREMENTS

Access to legal counsel is an important civil right in the U.S. legal system. Because the practice of law affects the general welfare of society, all states require attorneys to be licensed and credentialed. To practice law, an attorney must pass a bar exam and follow various professional ethics and regulations. Because they work under the supervision of an attorney, paralegals also must comply with certain laws and ethics.

A LICENSE IS NOT REQUIRED

Unlike attorneys, paralegals do not need a license to work as a paralegal. Some state legislatures have considered adopting regulations governing paralegal work. Proposed state laws have included requiring licensing, certification, or registration for paralegals. No state has established any type of regulatory program for paralegals.

Although paralegals are not regulated, they can voluntarily take a test to demonstrate their expertise at paralegal work. The NFPA administers two different tests. Its Paralegal CORE Competency Exam (PCCE) allows entry-level paralegals to demonstrate their competency. Its Paralegal Advanced Competency Examination (PACE) enables experienced paralegals to demonstrate their advanced skills and expertise. The state bar associations of Ohio and North Carolina have developed their own voluntary paralegal competency exams. The Texas Board of Legal Specialization Paralegal Certification Program has a certification process for paralegals in six specific legal fields.

Paralegals take these voluntary exams to strengthen their credentials. Many paralegals entering the field view the PCCE as an important credential that will help get them a job. In an interview with *U.S. News and World Report*, Tracey Young, former president of the NFPA, stated, "By successfully passing a voluntary certification exam such as the Paralegal CORE Competency Exam, candidates demonstrate their knowledge and understanding of the essential skills and concepts necessary to effectively work as a paralegal."

THE REGULATION DEBATE

Those who support regulating paralegals point out that regulation could provide many benefits. It would establish minimum standards for the paralegal profession. It would help distinguish qualified paralegals from unqualified paralegals. Regulation would also protect legal clients from potential malpractice from unqualified paralegals. Those opposed to regulation of paralegals argue that paralegals are already supervised by licensed attorneys, who are responsible for their work. Attorneys have no incentive to employ unqualified paralegals. Opponents also point out that regulation would increase the cost of legal services.

All states have statutes prohibiting anyone who is not a member of the state bar association from providing legal advice or representing someone in legal matters. Such laws are known as unlicensed-to-practice laws. These laws protect the public from being harmed by unqualified legal practitioners. People who cannot afford legal services sometimes seek legal advice from nonlawyers. These advisers often provide poor legal counsel, which makes their clients' legal problems worse. The laws forbidding the unlicensed practice of law cover paralegals. Although paralegals perform a wide range of legal tasks, they must avoid any work that constitutes the practice of law.

Exactly what constitutes the practice of law is unclear. In a 1922 case, the California Supreme Court adopted this definition of the practice of law:

> the practice of the law is the doing and performing services in a court of justice, in any matter depending therein, throughout its various stages, and in conformity to the adopted rules of procedure. But in a larger sense it includes legal advice and counsel, and the preparation of legal instruments and contracts by which legal rights are secured although such matter may or may not be depending in a court.

Aspiring paralegals take a competency exam. Although no state requires certification for paralegals, passing a paralegal certification exam boosts the credentials of job applicants seeking a paralegal position.

As paralegals have taken on more responsibilities over the years, the issue of what constitutes the practice of law has become more of a problem for attorneys, paralegals, and bar associations. State laws and bar association rules provide some guidance to attorneys and paralegals, but the boundaries have not been clearly defined.

Courts and bar associations have designated several activities as inappropriate for a paralegal. A paralegal may not establish an attorney-client relationship. He or she cannot tell a client that an attorney will or will not represent the client. A paralegal,

ETHICS COURSES

Because the boundaries of the legal tasks performed by paralegals are expanding today, paralegals must maintain a complete understanding of current professional ethics. Most paralegal education programs introduce students to the basic ethical standards of the paralegal field. Paralegals may also consult bar association and paralegal association ethical rules for guidance. NFPA and NALA recommend that paralegals continue ethics training throughout their careers.

however, may inform prospective clients of the attorney's decision about whether that attorney will represent the clients. A paralegal also cannot negotiate the terms of an attorney-client relationship. A paralegal cannot give oral or written legal advice or opinion to a client. She can relay advice and information from the attorney to the client but cannot state a legal opinion or advice. Paralegals must be careful not to give informal legal advice to friends or family members. A paralegal cannot interpret a legal document for a client. A paralegal cannot appear in any court hearing for a client, except in certain circumstances authorized by state or federal law.

An attorney (second from right) *discusses a client's case with two paralegals. Although an attorney is ultimately responsible for the paralegal's work, a paralegal must maintain client confidentiality and notify a supervising attorney of any conflict of interest with a client's case.*

State laws and bar association regulations allow lawyers to employ paralegals and delegate tasks to them. The attorney must supervise the paralegal's work and is responsible for that work. Paralegals may perform an extensive range of legal tasks while avoiding practicing law. They may draft a contract, but the attorney must review the contract before presenting it to a client. Paralegals may inform a client about a settlement offer but cannot advise the client whether to accept the offer. Paralegals may assist in preparing a case for court and assist an attorney at trial, but they may not appear in court as the client's advocate.

PROFESSIONAL RESPONSIBILITY

Many paralegals are members of national, state, or local paralegal associations. Many of these associations have established codes of ethics for their members. Member paralegals must follow these ethical rules, which are usually similar to state bar association ethical rules that govern the conduct of attorneys.

Paralegal ethic codes usually require paralegals to maintain a high level of competence at their jobs and to maintain personal and professional integrity. They must maintain a high standard of professional conduct. A paralegal must disclose his or her status and title to clients and other parties involved in the client's case to avoid any assumption that he is an attorney representing a client. A paralegal must preserve all of a client's confidential information.

A paralegal must avoid conflicts of interest. For example, if a prospective client seeks to pursue a lawsuit against a member of the paralegal's family, the paralegal must disclose the conflict of interest to the supervising attorney.

A volunteer paralegal (right) interviews a New Orleans man left homeless because of Hurricane Katrina. Paralegals often provide pro bono, or free, legal work to help their communities by assisting people who cannot afford legal services.

State bar association rules require lawyers to provide free legal services to deserving individuals who cannot afford them. These free legal services are usually called *pro bono publico*, from the Latin phrase meaning "for the public good." This requirement is seen as part of a lawyer's duty to the legal profession. State bar association and paralegal associations also encourage paralegals to participate in pro bono legal service programs.

chapter 6

PURSUING A PARALEGAL CAREER

More than 250,000 paralegals work in the United States, according to the U.S. Bureau of Labor Statistics (BLS). They work in many different types of organizations. The vast majority of paralegals work for a law firm, a corporate legal department, or a government agency. The paralegal field has gained a reputation for being an expanding employment sector offering many opportunities. Competition for paralegal jobs has increased because more people are training for paralegal careers. Finding a job in the field can be challenging for those entering the profession.

EMPLOYERS

Paralegals work for many different types of employers. Some paralegals work for private practice attorneys. These attorneys are sometimes called sole practitioners because they operate a one-attorney law office. Many sole practitioners limit their business to only a few legal fields. Some private practice attorneys specialize in just one field, such as criminal law. In this type of law office, a paralegal usually works on most, if not all, of the attorney's cases. The paralegal may also have more clerical and administrative responsibilities because one-attorney offices usually have fewer legal secretaries or other support staff.

Some attorneys work in small practices known as partnerships. The attorneys practice together in a group of two or more. Some partnerships specialize in a specific legal field, which allows the partners to work closely together. A paralegal working in a partnership may work for one partner or for several partners, depending on how the partnership is organized.

Large law firms have many attorneys. Because of their size, large law firms usually have attorneys who specialize in many different legal fields. For example, in a law firm, one attorney may specialize in real estate law, another in business law, and yet another in international law. All of these specialists can handle all of the legal problems of a client, such as a large corporation, within the same firm. Law firms are usually set up like corporations. Law firms generally employ many paralegals and support staff. A paralegal in a large law firm may work with an individual attorney. They may also work for a group of

A supervising attorney (center) listens to a paralegal discussing a client's case with other paralegals. Paralegals often work together to help the supervising attorney resolve a client's legal issue or problem.

attorneys who specialize in a specific legal field. Some paralegals in law firms may focus their work on a specific phase of the firm's cases. A paralegal, for instance, may be in charge of all field investigations or be responsible for the filing of all the firm's court documents.

Private practice attorneys, partnerships, and law firms are not the only parties that employ paralegals. Many large companies, such as Apple and Ford Motor Company, have their own legal departments. Attorneys working in corporate legal departments are known as in-house counsel. A paralegal working in a corporate legal department is likely to specialize in a field related to the company's business. For example, a paralegal working for a large airline may specialize in transportation law.

Government agencies at the federal, state, and local levels also employ paralegals. For example, the Environmental Protection Agency has a legal staff that enforces federal

A paralegal working for a charity helps an immigrant prepare the paperwork required for legal immigration status. Legal immigration status will allow the woman to work in the United States legally and to receive health and other services provided by charities and government agencies.

environmental laws and regulations. Prosecutors and district attorneys at all levels of government employ lawyers and paralegals. These government lawyers enforce state and local criminal laws. Paralegals working for government agencies often specialize in a field of law, such as housing law or food safety law.

FINDING A PARALEGAL JOB

Finding your first job in the paralegal field can be an intimidating task. Although the demand for paralegal services remains high, the competition for jobs is intense. This fierce competitiveness is especially true for those seeking a paralegal job for the first time. To get a leg up, it helps if you have some experience in paralegal work, either through participation in an internship or as a temporary worker. It also helps if you follow basic job search guidelines.

For most prospective paralegals, the first step after earning their paralegal studies certificate or degree is to create a résumé. Job seekers use a résumé to showcase their skills, experience, and accomplishments. The résumé is an indispensable tool for marketing your skills to legal employers. It is the first contact you have with a potential employer. You want to make a good first impression, so your résumé should be designed to catch a hiring manager's attention.

You should tailor your résumé to your own background and to the paralegal job you seek. A résumé for a paralegal position should contain several basic elements. Your name and contact information should appear at the top. You want to present your strongest credentials first. If you have worked in the legal field or a related field, list and describe your job experience first. Your work history should provide your full-time, part-time, summer, temp, and volunteer jobs. It should include a description of each job's responsibilities and your accomplishments

Lucia X. Rivera
840 W. Main Street
Grant, Indiana
Home: (555) 555-2481 Cell: (555) 555-9953
lxrivera@grantnet.com

Objective: Highly motivated and detail-oriented college graduate seeks a paralegal position in a law firm specializing in family law.

Education

Certificate in Paralegal Studies
Hilltop College, 2014
Concentration in family law and litigation

B.A. in Social Work
Western State University, 2012

Experience

Intern
Patton & Meeks, LLC
Performed paralegal duties under the supervision of an attorney and certified paralegal
January–April 2012

Intern
Central County Children and Family Services
Assisted social workers on child neglect and abuse cases
September–December 2012

Library Assistant
Western State University Library
Fall and spring semesters, 2008–2012 (work-study program)

Volunteer Library Assistant
Grant Public Library
June–August 2008

Other skills

Proficient in PC use; spreadsheet and word-processing programs
Familiar with Lexis/Nexis and other legal research tools

Awards and activities

Dean's List, Hilltop College, 2008–2012

References available on request

This sample shows many of the basic elements that a résumé for a recent graduate of a paralegal studies certificate program should provide. Creating an effective résumé is a crucial part of landing a paralegal job offer.

and the skills you learned at the job. If you have little work experience, it may be best to highlight your educational background first. You should include all the educational institutions you have attended. You should list the degrees and awards you have earned, along with any certifications and internships. The contents of the résumé must be factual. Exaggerating your accomplishments may backfire.

The goal of a résumé is to convey your skills and background effectively to a potential employer. When designing your résumé, you should make sure it is easy to read. It is best to use a common, basic font and avoid dense chunks of text. Proofread your résumé to make certain that it contains no errors. Check spellings carefully, and do not rely on your word-processing software's spell-checker. When printing out your résumé, use a neutral white or cream-colored paper.

After perfecting your résumé, the next step is to search for a job. Your paralegal certificate or degree program may offer placement services to help graduates find jobs. Employers advertise jobs on online job sites (such as Indeed.com, Monster .com, and Craigslist.org) and in local newspaper ads. Some job-listing Web sites specialize in legal positions. Job candidates can also approach law firms and law firms directly. State and local bar associations, directories listing lawyers and law firms, and even the phone book are sources of contact information. You should approach corporations, nonprofits, and government agencies, particularly if you have background in their field.

Networking is often a successful way to discover job openings. If you had an internship, discuss job opportunities with the firm's hiring manager, paralegal supervisor, or attorneys you assisted. If the firm does not have a current position available, someone may know another attorney or law firm looking for a paralegal. Approach lawyers you know. You can also find leads by speaking with your paralegal studies instructors, friends, and family members. Expand your network by asking all of these people to put you in contact with their friends and colleagues who may have leads on paralegal jobs. Using LinkedIn, Facebook, and other social networking Web sites is another way to make useful employment contacts.

At a university-sponsored job fair, a paralegal student listens as a representative from a government agency explains employment opportunities at her agency. Job fairs enable paralegal job seekers to meet with different types of prospective employers.

While looking for a permanent job, some prospective paralegals take temporary paralegal jobs. Temporary work allows you to get more experience as a paralegal and provide an income while conducting your search for a permanent job. It also gives

you a chance to impress your temporary employer. These temporary assignments sometimes lead to an offer for a full-time position.

Once you have found a job opening that appeals to you, the next step is to apply for the position. Read the job listing carefully and follow the instructions exactly. The listing may ask you to mail or e-mail your résumé. In either case, include a cover letter. A cover letter is a standard business letter that accompanies a résumé. It allows you to introduce yourself to the employer. Its main purpose is to show employers that your skills and background are appropriate for the job they are seeking to fill. A cover letter should be personalized and written so that it focuses on the specific position you're applying for. A cover letter should always make the case that you are the best person for the job. Like your résumé, your cover letter should be short, concise, and free of errors.

When your résumé and cover letter catch the eye of a hiring

SELF-EMPLOYED PARALEGALS

Some experienced paralegals work as independent contractors, also known as freelancers. Attorneys and law firms sometimes need short-term paralegal services for specific cases, during specific seasons, or for specific purposes. For instance, a firm handling a large, complex case may need a freelance paralegal to help its support staff prepare evidence for an upcoming trial.

Self-employed paralegals are hired to perform assigned tasks under the supervision of an attorney. They are not employees of the attorney or a law firm. They are paid an agreed-upon flat rate or an hourly fee for their services. Self-employment may be an attractive option for paralegals who want to work part-time, have other life commitments, are pursuing a career change, or approaching retirement age.

manager, the employer may contact you to schedule an interview. The interview allows the employer to ask you in-depth questions about your education and employment background. It also gives the employer a chance to assess your poise and professionalism. A job interview also provides the best opportunity for you to convince the employer that you are the ideal candidate for the job.

A job interview can be stressful, but the candidates who get hired are the ones who were prepared for their interview. They arrive at the employer's office on time. They wear professional clothes that are appropriate for a law office. They are well groomed. Successful job applicants are prepared to ask the employer questions about the job and the firm. They always thank the people who interview them. If you are still interested in the job after the interview, follow up with a brief handwritten letter thanking the interviewer and expressing your genuine interest in the position.

Career books and online sources provide a wealth of information for job seekers. Consult these sources to help you with the paralegal job search process. They will also provide tips on writing résumés and cover letters and on how to prepare for and succeed at job interviews.

THE WORK ENVIRONMENT

Paralegals do most of their work in law offices and law libraries. They sometimes work outside of the office, conducting investigations, interviewing witnesses, and delivering documents. Most paralegals work under the direct supervision of a lawyer in a legal practice or law firm. Some larger firms appoint experienced paralegals as paralegal managers or coordinators. Other

A paralegal who works for a nonprofit organization assists a man who faces eviction from his home. Some nonprofits employ paralegals to help the organization carry out its mission to help individuals and communities.

paralegals work under the supervision of a lawyer who does not work in a law firm. Corporations, governments, nonprofits, and other organizations employ these paralegals. Some government paralegals are authorized by law to represent clients in government agency proceedings. The Social Security Act, for instance, allows paralegals to represent certain people at hearings involving disability insurance.

Paralegals who work for law firms, corporations, and government agencies usually work full-time. They may work very long hours and sometimes work overtime to meet deadlines. In *Paralegal Today*, paralegal Jean Cushman advised, "It's important to find a group of attorneys and support staff you are compatible with. It really is a team effort and you need to be compatible with the individuals you will be working with."

What individual paralegals do on a day-to-day basis often depends on their employer and their specific job. For example, corporate paralegals often help prepare contracts and financial reports. They may also review government regulations to make sure the corporation is in compliance with the law. In contrast, litigation paralegals at large law firms may focus their work on handling client documents, conducting legal research, and organizing evidence for trial.

chapter 7

EMPLOYMENT OUTLOOK FOR PARALEGALS

The paralegal profession appears to have a bright future. Attorneys, law firms, and other legal employers are expected to increase their hiring of paralegals. Many large law firms reduced their staffs following the 2007–2008 financial crisis. As the economy started recovering, these firms began rehiring to meet the increased demand for legal services. They responded by hiring greater numbers of paralegals.

FACTORS IN JOB GROWTH

Because paralegals can perform a wide range of legal tasks that attorneys perform, they provide law firms with a less expensive alternative to hiring additional attorneys. Unlike some other legal positions, paralegal work is difficult to offshore outsource to other countries. Some of the tasks performed by paralegals must be performed in person. For example, a paralegal must handle court documents and interview witnesses, which cannot be done by a worker abroad. Paralegals often meet with clients and other parties involved in a case. They also work alongside attorneys to organize information and documents for court hearings and business transactions.

A real estate agent discusses the details of a home offered for sale with his clients. Gaining experience in legal work gives paralegals the knowledge and skills to make a change to a career in many other fields, including real estate.

ALTERNATIVE CAREERS

The work of a paralegal gives a person the experience and skills to pursue other careers. Accomplished paralegals may be qualified to move into other positions inside their employer's firms, such as hiring managers, litigation support managers, and computer technology consultants. Experienced paralegals may be qualified for a variety of positions in the legal field. Other career choices for paralegals include real estate brokers, investigators, mediators, arbitrators, special advocates, and estate and trust officers.

Some paralegals also become lawyers. After working in the field, these paralegals decide to attend law school, either part-time or full-time, to advance their legal career. Some prospective law students decide to spend a few years working as a paralegal before applying to law school. This work experience increases their chances of being admitted to the law school of their choice. Their background

THE IMPORTANCE OF SPECIALIZATION

Specialization is becoming common in the paralegal field. Paralegals can often command a higher salary and have better job security if they specialize in a specific legal field. By specializing in a legal field, a paralegal acquires a large amount of knowledge about the laws in that field. With more experience and knowledge in the field, a specialist paralegal can provide better legal services more efficiently. Specialization is good for the client and for the law firm. Popular specialized paralegal fields include litigation, bankruptcy, corporate law, intellectual property, and real estate law.

in the practical application of the law helps them understand their academic studies in law school.

JOB OUTLOOK

The U.S. Department of Labor expects job opportunities for paralegals to expand greatly. In 2009, the BLS estimated that the paralegal employment sector would grow by 18 percent between 2010 and 2020. The BLS also provides a salary outlook for the position of paralegal. For the latest salary outlook, refer to the BLS (http://www.bls.gov/ooh/Legal/Paralegals -and-legal-assistants.htm).

The BLS cautions that this expected growth in employment opportunity for paralegals will be accompanied by increased competition for jobs. Because of the many benefits and rewards that a paralegal career offers, the BLS expects more people to

A recent paralegal studies graduate meets with a prospective employer. The U.S. Department of Labor predicts that the future growth of paralegal jobs will outpace the average job increase in all employment fields combined.

enter the profession. Experienced, trained paralegals are likely to have better employment prospects than inexperienced, untrained candidates. In an interview with *U.S. News and World Report*, former NFPA president Tracey Young recommended that paralegal job seekers "join a local paralegal association to network and get an inside track on employment opportunities." She also advised employed paralegals to volunteer for pro bono opportunities to get additional practical experience.

glossary

accredit To recognize as maintaining adequate educational standards.

adversarial Involving two sides that oppose each other.

affidavit A written report signed by a person who pledges that the information is true.

appellate Being concerned with or dealing with applications for decisions to be reversed.

arbitrator A person who settles a dispute.

attorney A person who provides legal advice and representation.

bar association An organization of attorneys, whose members are allowed to practice in a given state.

case law A law based on decisions that judges have made in previous cases.

conflict of interest Whenever the professional and personal interests of a person clash.

constitution A document that states the basic principles used to govern a state or country.

deposition A formal statement made under oath before a trial by a witness.

due process The procedures in the judicial system that respect the rights of individuals.

ethics Rules that define good behavior.

legal assistant A person who assists an attorney by performing legal tasks; a paralegal.

mediator A person who works with opposing sides to settle a dispute.

motion A formal request made to a court of law for something to be done, such as delaying a hearing.

offshore outsource To relocate a business or department, in particular, information technology-related work, to a foreign country to take advantage of lower costs.

paralegal A person who assists an attorney by performing legal tasks; a legal assistant.

pleading A formal, written statement made by a party in a court case.

precedent A decision, such as a court case, that serves as an example to be followed in the future.

pro bono Free legal services.

settlement An agreement to resolve a legal dispute before going to trial.

special advocate A nonlawyer appointed by a court or authorized by a statute to represent a person before a court or regulatory agency.

statute A law passed by a legislature.

will A legal document in which a person states who should receive his or her possessions after he or she dies.

American Association for Paralegal Education
19 Mantua Road
Mount Royal, NJ 08061
(856) 423-2829
Web site: http://www.aafpe.org
This nonprofit provides information for students interested in
    paralegal education programs.

American Bar Association
Standing Committee on Paralegals
321 North Clark Street
Chicago, IL 60654
(312) 988-5000
Web site: http://www.americanbar.org/groups/paralegals.html
This attorney membership organization provides career and
    educational resources for paralegals.

Bureau of Labor Statistics
Division of Information and Marketing Services
2 Massachusetts Avenue NE, Room 2850
Washington, DC 20212
(202) 691-5200
Web site: http://www.bls.gov
This government agency within the U.S. Department of
    Labor provides information on paralegal work, as well
    as employment and salary outlooks in its online career
    reference *Occupational Outlook Handbook* (http://
    www.bls.gov/ooh/Legal/Paralegals-and-legal
    -assistants.htm).

Canadian Association of Paralegals
2606 Adhémar-Raynault Avenue
L'Assomption, QC J5W 0E1
Canada
Web site: http://www.caplegal.ca
This nonprofit organization supplies information and
resources for paralegals and paralegal studies students in
Canada.

Canadian Bar Association
500-865 Carling Avenue
Ottawa, ON K1S 5S8
Canada
(613) 237-2925
Web site: http://www.cba.org/cba
The Canadian Bar Association is an attorney membership
organization that offers career and educational resources
for Canadian paralegals.

CriminalJusticePrograms.com
15500 West 113th Street, Suite 200
Lenexa, KS 66219
(877) 412-6411
Web site: http://www.criminaljusticeprograms.com/specialty
/paralegal
This Web site provides listing of institutions that provide
paralegal education courses, certification programs, and
degree programs.

Federal Student Aid
P.O. Box 84
Washington, DC 20044
(800) 433-3243
Web site: http://www.studentaid.ed.gov

An agency within the U.S. Department of Education, Federal
    Student Aid supplies information on various federal stu-
    dent loan programs.

Legal Talk Network
3120 Blake Street
Denver, CO 80205
(800) 753-1844
Web site: http://www.legaltalknetwork.com/about/our
    -programs/the-paralegal-voice
This media company broadcasts "Paralegal Voice," a monthly
    podcast that discusses trends and issues relevant to
    paralegals.

Los Angeles Paralegal Association
P.O. Box 71708
Los Angeles, CA 90071
(866) 626-5272
Web site: http://www.lapa.org
This nonprofit professional association provides information for
    and about paralegals in the Los Angeles metropolitan area.

National Association of Legal Assistants
1516 S. Boston, #200
Tulsa, OK 74119
(918) 587-6828
Web site: http://www.nala.org
This nonprofit paralegal association provides publications,
    news, job information, and other resources for paralegals.

National Federation of Paralegal Associations
23607 Highway 99, Suite 2-C
Edmonds, WA 98026

(425) 967-0045
Web site: http://www.paralegals.org
This professional association provides publications and other
information about the paralegal profession.

North Carolina Paralegal Association
P.O. Box 36264
Charlotte, NC 28236
(704) 535-3363
Web site: http://www.ncparalegal.org
This nonprofit professional association provides a career
center for North Carolina paralegals and paralegal
students.

Paralegal Today
Conexion International Media, Inc.
6030 Marshalee Drive, Suite 455
Elkridge, MD 21075-5935
(443) 445-3057
Web site: http://paralegaltoday.com
This magazine provides paralegals with news, salary data, and
other professional information.

WEB SITES

Due to the changing nature of Internet links, Rosen Publishing
has developed an online list of Web sites related to the subject
of this book. This site is updated regularly. Please use this link
to access the list:

http://www.rosenlinks.com/EC/Legal

for further reading

Bolles, Richard. *What Color Is Your Parachute: A Practical Manual for Job-Hunters and Job-Changers*. New York, NY: Crown/Random House, 2013.

Bouchoux, Deborah E. *Legal Research & Writing for Paralegals*. New York, NY: Aspen, 2011.

Currier, Katherine A., and Thomas E. Eimermann. *Introduction to Law for Paralegals*. New York, NY: Aspen, 2011.

Elias, Stephen. *Legal Research: How to Find & Understand the Law*. Berkeley, CA: Nolo, 2012.

Goldman, Thomas F., and Henry R. Cheeseman. *The Paralegal Professional*. Upper Saddle River, NJ: Prentice Hall, 2010.

Hatch, Scott, and Lisa Zimmer Hatch. *Paralegal Procedures and Practices*. Albany, NY: Delmar, 2009.

Haworth, Anita, and Leslie G. Cox. *The Paralegal's Handbook*. New York, NY: Kaplan Publishing, 2010.

Kennedy, Joyce Lain. *Cover Letters for Dummies*. Hoboken, NJ: Wiley Publishing, 2009.

Kennedy, Joyce Lain. *Job Interviews for Dummies*. Hoboken, NJ: Wiley Publishing, 2011.

Kennedy, Joyce Lain. *Résumés for Dummies*. Hoboken, NJ: Wiley Publishing, 2011.

Larbalestrie, Deborah E. *Paralegal Practice and Procedure*. Upper Saddle River, NJ: Prentice Hall, 2009.

Learning Express editors. *Becoming a Paralegal*. New York, NY: Learning Express, 2010.

Miller, Roger, and Mary Meinzinger. *Paralegal Today: The Essentials*. Albany, NY: Delmar, 2010.

Miller, Roger, and Mary Meinzinger. *Paralegal Today: The Legal Team at Work*. Albany, NY: Delmar, 2013.

National Association of Legal Assistants. *NALA Manual for Paralegals and Legal Assistants*. Albany, NY: Delmar, 2009.

Newman, Virginia Koerselman. *Certified Paralegal Review Manual: A Practical Guide to CP Exam Preparation*. Albany, NY: Delmar, 2010.

Samborn, Hope Viner, and Andrea Banchik Yelin. *Basic Legal Writing for Paralegals*. New York, NY: Aspen, 2012.

U.S. Department of Labor. *Occupational Outlook Handbook, 2013–2014*. New York, NY: Skyhorse Publishing, 2012.

Wagner, Andrea. *How to Land Your First Paralegal Job*. Upper Saddle River, NJ: Prentice Hall, 2009.

Yellin, Andrea Banchik, and Hope Viner Samborn. *The Legal Research and Writing Handbook*. 6th ed. New York, NY: Aspen, 2011.

bibliography

Bouchoux, Deborah E. *Legal Research & Writing for Paralegals.* New York, NY: Aspen, 2011.

Campbell, Rachel. "Advice from Experienced Paralegals." Retrieved March 11, 2013 (http://paralegaltoday.com/issue_archive/features/feature1_jf04.htm).

Campbell, Rachel. "A Look at Paralegal Employment Options." Retrieved March 11, 2013 (http://paralegaltoday.com/issue_archive/features/feature_ma04.htm).

Chin, Linda T. "Writing Paralegal Resumes." Retrieved March 11, 2013 (http://paralegaltoday.com/issue_archive/online_only/paralegal_resumes.htm).

CNN/Money. "Best Jobs in America: Paralegal." Retrieved March 10, 2013 (http://money.cnn.com/galleries/2007/moneymag/0703/gallery.bestjobs_young.moneymag/14.html).

Creekmore, Mary L. "Top Essential Skills and Assets for Paralegals." Retrieved March 20, 2013 (http://www.law.com/jsp/pa/PubArticlePA.jsp?id=1202441952307).

CriminalJusticePrograms.com. "Paralegal Degrees and Careers: California." Retrieved March 11, 2013 (http://www.criminaljusticeprograms.com/specialty/paralegal/#california).

Elias, Stephen. *Legal Research: How to Find & Understand the Law.* Berkeley, CA: Nolo, 2012.

Kane, Sally A. "Take Your Seats: A Front-Row Look at Trends in Paralegal Training and Programs." Retrieved March 11, 2013 (http://paralegaltoday.com/issue_archive/features/feature1_jf09.htm)

Learning Express editors. *Becoming a Paralegal.* New York, NY: Learning Express, 2010.

Los Angeles County Office of the District Attorney. "Unauthorized Practice of Law: Manual for Prosecutors." Retrieved March 10, 2013 (http://da.co.la.ca.us/pdf /UPLpublic.pdf).

National Association of Legal Assistants. "About Paralegals." Retrieved March 11, 2013 (http://www.nala.org /AboutParalegals.aspx).

National Association of Legal Assistants. "Certification." Retrieved March 11, 2013 (http://www.nala.org /Certification.aspx).

National Association of Legal Assistants. "Paralegal Educational Programs." Retrieved March 11, 2013 (http://www.nala.org/paralegaleducation.aspx).

National Federation of Paralegal Associations. "The Ethical Wall: Its Application to Paralegals." Retrieved March 12, 2013 (http://www.paralegals.org/associations/2270/files /THE_ETHICAL_WALL.pdf).

National Federation of Paralegal Associations. "Model Code of Ethics and Professional Responsibility and Guidelines for Enforcement." Retrieved March 12, 2013 (http://www. paralegals.org/associations/2270/files/Model_Code _of_Ethics_09_06.pdf).

National Federation of Paralegal Associations. "Model Plan for Paralegal Licensure." Retrieved March 12, 2013 (http://www.paralegals.org/associations/2270/files /Licensed_Paralegal_Plan.pdf).

National Federation of Paralegal Associations. "Paralegals and Conflicts of Interest." Retrieved March 12, 2013 (http:// www.paralegals.org/default.asp?page=70).

National Federation of Paralegal Associations. "Paralegal Responsibilities." Retrieved March 12, 2013

(http://www.paralegals.org/associations/2270/files
/Paralegal_Responsibilities.pdf).

Schneider, Steven. *The Everything Guide to Being a Paralegal: Winning Secrets to a Successful Career.* Avon, MA: Adams Media, 2006.

U.S. News and World Report. "Best Social Service Jobs: Paralegal." Retrieved March 11, 2013 (http://money .usnews.com/careers/best-jobs/paralegal).

index

ABOUT THE AUTHOR

G. S. Prentzas has written more than thirty books for young people. He also writes articles on legal topics for Lawyers.com, LegalZoom.com, and other Web sites. He graduated with an A.B. degree in English with honors and a J.D. degree with honors from the University of North Carolina School of Law.

PHOTO CREDITS

Cover (figure) © iStockphoto.com/EHStock; cover (background), p. 1 © iStockphoto.com/Eliza Snow; pp. 4, 20, 28–29 iStockphoto/Thinkstock; p. 8 U.S. National Archives and Records Administration; p. 9 Ron Chapple/Taxi/Getty Images; pp. 10–11 Bruce Ayres/Stone/Getty Images; p. 12 McClatchy-Tribune/Getty Images; pp. 16–17 James Nielsen/AFP/Getty Images; p. 18 The Washington Post/Getty Images; p. 22 PNC/Photodisc/Getty Images; p. 25 Dave and Les Jacobs/Blend Images/Getty Images; p. 27 Image Source/Getty Images; pp. 31, 51 Yuri Arcurs/Shutterstock.com; pp. 34, 40 © AP Images; p. 37 Chris Schmidt/E+/Getty Images; p. 44 wavebreakmedia/Shutterstock.com; p. 46 Digital Vision/Thinkstock; pp. 48–49 New York Daily News Archive/Getty Images; p. 52 © Sun-Sentinel/ZUMA Press; pp. 56–57 © Augusta Chronicle/ZUMA Press; p. 59 Sacramento Bee/Chris Crewell/ZUMA Press; pp. 62–63 Christian Kieffer/Shutterstock.com; p. 65 Ingram Publishing/Thinkstock; back cover (background) © iStockphoto.com/blackred.

Designer: Matt Cauli; Editor: Kathy Kuhtz Campbell; Photo Researcher: Karen Huang